Teacher Training Through

VIDEO

ESL
TECHNIQUES

PROBLEM SOLVING

SERIES EDITOR: K. LYNN SAVAGE
AUTHORS: LEANN HOWARD
LINDA LITTLE

Longman

Teacher Training Through Video: Problem Solving

Longman, 95 Church Street, White Plains, N.Y. 10601

Associated companies:
Longman Group Ltd., London
Longman Cheshire Pty., Melbourne
Longman Paul Pty., Auckland
Copp Clark Pitman, Toronto

This work was originally developed by the ESL Teacher
Institute, Association of California School Administrators,
Foundation for Educational Administration, under a state-
administered contract of the Federal P.L. 100-297, Section
353, from the California State Department of Education,
721 Capitol Mall, Sacramento, California 95814. However,
the content does not necessarily reflect the position or
policy of that department or the United States Department
of Education. No official endorsement of this work should
be inferred.

*Photo/text credits: The Resource Material in the "Guided Practice"
section is reprinted with permission.*

Problem Solving by Linda W. Little and Ingrid A. Greenberg.
Copyright ©1991, Longman, p. 95.

Distributed in the United Kingdom by Longman Group
Ltd., Longman House, Burnt Mill, Harlow, Essex CM20
2JE, England and by associated companies, branches,
and representatives throughout the world.

Executive editor: Joanne Dresner
Development editor: Penny Laporte
Production editor: Helen B. Ambrosio
Text design: Publication Services
Cover design: Design-5

ISBN 0-8013-0739-2 Workbook
ISBN 0-8013-0729-5 Reproducible Masters

1 2 3 4 5 6 7 8 9 10 - AL - 9594939291

Contents

- Introduction **iv**
- Training Goal and Objectives **1**
- Background Information **2**
- Video Demonstration **5**
- Classroom Observation **9**
- Guided Practice **13**
- Application **19**
- Appendix **24**
- Acknowledgments **27**
- Titles in the Teacher Training Through Video Series **28**

Introduction

Teacher Training Through Video: ESL Techniques is a series of ten interactive teaching videos. Each video has supporting instructional material available as reproducible masters or workbooks.

Each set in the series consists of (1) a videotaped demonstration of a specific technique or strategy and (2) reproducible masters (also available as workbooks).

Each set reflects the key elements in teacher training, i.e., presentation of goals and principles of a technique, multiple models of the technique, practicing the technique, transference of skills to the classroom, and flexibility of training time.

Each of the reproducible masters/workbooks is organized into the following format:

■ *Training Goal and Objectives* provides an overview of the material. The training goal is a statement of the skills intended for trainees who complete the material. In order to attain that goal, trainees complete each of the objectives listed under the training objectives.

■ *Background Information* presents the theory and research related to the specific technique. It also discusses implications for instruction. It assists trainees in making sound decisions about when it is appropriate to use the skills on which the material focuses. This section is divided into four parts: focus questions, a short reading, follow-up questions, and a bibliography of professional references for further reading.

■ The *Video Demonstration/Classroom Observation* provides two models of the technique.

The first model is presented through a Video Demonstration. Each video shows an actual class in which the teacher uses the technique. Print materials provide an introduction to the video. This introduction, or Lesson Focus, presents basic information about the class on the video (level, length, number of students, etc.) as well as the lesson (topic, objective, basic and life skill focus, language skill focus).

It is followed by a Feedback Form to be completed while watching the video. The Feedback Form is used throughout the printed material: to guide the observation and discussion of the video demonstration and the classroom demonstration; to guide development of the trainee's own lessons; and to analyze the effectiveness of the trainee's own lessons.

The Feedback Form is a series of questions. These questions list the steps in the instructional strategy. The steps are sequenced. Beneath each question are options. Trainees indicate what they observed by checking the box beside each option observed and writing any relevant notes. The Feedback Forms are organized by stages: Warm-Up/Review, Introduction, Presentation, Practice, Evaluation, and Application. Two kinds of print are used on the forms. The boldfaced steps are key steps in the technique. The light face steps are key steps in any lesson, regardless of technique.

The Follow-Up to the Video Demonstration poses questions to encourage discussion of the technique and evaluation of the lesson.

The second model is through a Classroom Observation. The materials to accompany this activity mirror those designed for the video demonstration. The Lesson Focus requires trainees to obtain the same kind of information as presented in the Video Demonstration section. This may be obtained from the observation or from an interview of the instructor observed. This section also includes a copy of the Feedback Form, intended to be completed during the classroom observation. The Follow-Up allows time for discussing and evaluating the observation.

■ *Guided Practice* develops skills in using the technique. Resource materials taken from actual ESL textbooks are used as the instructional materials around which trainees practice using the technique. In each module there is one practice for each key step highlighted on the Feedback Form.

■ *Application* enables trainees to transfer the skills they have acquired through the reading, demonstrations, practices and discussions. The materials for this section consist of the Lesson Focus; the Lesson Plan, which lists the steps previously encountered as questions on the Feedback Form; the Feedback Form for trainees to use in analyzing their own lessons; and the Follow-Up, which asks questions to evaluate the lesson.

■ *The Appendix* material enables trainees to replicate in their own classrooms the lesson observed on the video. It includes the Video Instructional Materials and the Video Lesson Plan.

Each of the ten sets is designed to provide a minimum of four hours of formal training as well as five and a half to nine hours outside the formal training. The formal training includes an initial session or series of sessions which cover the following components of the workbooks: Background Information, Video Demonstration, and Practice. In addition, Classroom Observation and Application occur outside the formal training session and, for most effective use, should be followed by a formal discussion session.

Training Goal and Objectives

IIIIIIIIIIIIIIIIIIIIIIIIIIIIIIIIIIII

- *GOAL:*

  To develop skills in using the problem-solving technique

- *OBJECTIVES:*

  Upon completion of this module you will be able to

  1. Recognize the goals and underlying principles of the problem-solving technique

  2. Identify key steps in the problem-solving technique

  3. Provide students with an opportunity to identify the problem and discuss a variety of possible solutions and consequences

  4. Provide an activity in which individuals make their own choices and decisions

  5. Transform students' problems and concerns into a story

Background Information

▌▌▌▌▌▌▌▌▌▌▌▌▌▌▌▌▌▌▌▌▌▌│││││││││

The reading that follows gives a brief summary of the theory, research, teaching implications, and importance of the problem-solving technique.

┤┼┤┼┼┼┤•┤•┤▶ FOCUS QUESTIONS ▌▌▌▌▌▌▌▌▌▌▌▌▌▌▌▌▌▌▌▌▌▌▌▌▌▌▌▌▌▌▌▌▌▌▌│││││││

Read the focus questions. Then find the answers in the reading.

1. What does the problem-solving technique use as subjects for discussion?

   _____

   _____

2. What should be the atmosphere in a classroom that uses problem solving?

   _____

   _____

3. What is the role of grammar in the problem-solving technique?

   _____

   _____

4. What is the instructor's role in the problem-solving technique?

   _____

   _____

5. What is the sequence in a problem-solving discussion?

   _____

   _____

PROBLEM SOLVING

- ## *INSTRUCTIONAL GOAL:*

For students to develop critical thinking skills, problem-solving skills, and communicative competence

- ## *TARGET STUDENTS:*

Students who have intermediate-level fluency skills

The problem-solving technique helps develop communicative competence and the critical thinking and decision-making skills adults need to function effectively in everyday life. It uses the students' concerns and problems as subjects for discussion.

The problem-solving technique has been influenced by Freire's work on problem posing, Stevick's work on classroom climate, and Terrell's work on meaning (see the "Further Reading" section). The technique has several basic underlying principles:

1. Adult learners bring a great deal of experience and knowledge to the classroom. They learn best when their needs and interests are met and when they are involved in their own learning process.

2. Personal problems and concerns can interfere with the learning process. Addressing and discussing these problems and finding possible solutions can remove or reduce this interference.

3. In order for problem solving to work, each individual's culture and personal views need to be respected. The instructor must create a caring and supportive atmosphere in the classroom, an atmosphere in which everyone has a chance to talk and to be heard, or to remain silent.

4. During class discussions, the emphasis needs to be on the message, not on the form. Grammatical structures should not be emphasized at this time.

The role of the instructor is to listen to the students and transform their problems and concerns into a story, dialogue, or picture for class discussion. The instructor leads and facilitates the discussion, asking questions that will draw out the students. The discussion encourages students to do each of the following in the order listed:

1. Identify and think critically about the problem.

2. Discuss and examine the causes of the problem.

3. Identify a variety of possible solutions and their consequences in order to make informed choices.

4. Apply the problem to their own lives and experiences.

▬▶ FOLLOW-UP ▬▬▬▬▬▬▬▬▬▬▬

Think about the reading. Then answer the questions and discuss your answers.

1. How does the problem-solving technique help students make more informed choices and decisions?

    _____

    _____

    _____

2. Why is problem solving an appropriate technique for adults?

    _____

    _____

    _____

▬▶ FURTHER READING ▬▬▬▬▬▬▬▬▬▬▬

Brumfit, C. J., and Johnson, K., eds. *The Communicative Approach to Language Teaching.* Oxford: Oxford University Press, 1979.

Curran, Charles A. *Counseling-Learning.* New York: Grune and Stratton, 1972.

Farmer, J. A. "Adult Education for Transitioning." In *Paolo Freire: A Revolutionary Dilemma for the Adult Educator,* edited by Stanley Grabowski. ERIC Clearinghouse on Adult Education Occasional Paper #32, November 1972.

Freire, P. *Pedagogy of the Oppressed.* New York: The Seabury Press, 1970.

Krashen, Stephen. "Theory Versus Practice in Language Training." *Innovative Approaches to Language Teaching,* edited by R. W. Blair. Rowley, Mass.: Newbury House Publishers, 1976.

Stevick, F. W. *Memory, Meaning, and Method.* Rowley, Mass.: Newbury House Publishers, 1976.

Taba, H. "The Teaching of Thinking." *Elementary English* 42 (May 1965).

Taba, H., and Elkins, D. *Teaching Strategies for the Culturally Disadvantaged.* Chicago: Rand McNally and Company, 1966.

Terrell, T. "Natural Approach to Second Language Acquisition and Learning." *The Modern Language Journal* 61 (1977): pp. 325–337.

Wallerstein, W. *Language and Culture in Conflict.* Reading, Mass.: Addison-Wesley, 1983.

Teacher Training Through Video
Copyright©1992 by Longman Publishing Group

Video Demonstration

IIIIIIIIIIIIIIIIIIIIIIIIIIIIIIIIIIIIIIIII

The video demonstration presents a model of the problem-solving technique. There are three parts to the Video Demonstration section. The first part, *Lesson Focus,* presents basic information about the class on the video. The second part, *Feedback Form,* highlights the key steps in the technique as well as other steps present in an effective lesson. The third part, *Follow-Up,* encourages a better understanding of the technique through an analysis and discussion of the demonstration.

▶ LESSON FOCUS

Review the information below and the Feedback Form on pages 6 and 7. Then watch the video and complete the Feedback Form.

CLASS LEVEL: *Intermediate*

LENGTH OF CLASS: *1 hour 25 minutes*   NUMBER OF STUDENTS: *35*

LOCATION: *East San Diego Center*   INSTRUCTOR: *Linda Little*

TOPIC: *Employment and moving*

OBJECTIVE: The students will be able to *identify the problems, consequences, and possible solutions associated with accepting or declining a promotion that requires a move*

BASIC SKILLS (Language):

Critical thinking skills and discussion skills such as clarifying, expressing opinion, agreeing, and disagreeing.

LIFE SKILLS (Content): *Accepting or declining a promotion*

MAJOR SKILLS: (Listening)   (Speaking)   Reading   Writing

▶ FEEDBACK FORM ··· PROBLEM SOLVING

*Each question on the form refers to a step in the teaching process. For each question, decide whether you observed the behavior. If so, indicate what was observed by checking the appropriate box(es). Key steps in the technique are in **boldface**.*

WARM-UP/REVIEW

1. Did the instructor relate the lesson objective to previous learning?   YES   NO
   If so, how?
   - ☐ by having students practice previously studied material
   - ☐ by providing a warm-up activity
   - ☐ other _____

INTRODUCTION

2. Did the instructor focus student attention on the lesson?   YES   NO
   If so, how?
   - ☐ by using visuals and/or realia
   - ☐ by asking questions
   - ☐ by describing a situation
   - ☐ by telling a story
   - ☐ other _____

3. Did the instructor establish the purpose of the lesson?   YES   NO
   If so, how?
   - ☐ by stating the lesson objective
   - ☐ by relating the lesson objective to the students' own lives
   - ☐ other _____

PRESENTATION

4. **Was a problem situation provided?**   YES   NO
   If so, how?
   - ☐ by using visuals and/or realia
   - ☐ by explaining or describing
   - ☐ by asking questions
   - ☐ other _____

5. Did the instructor work with the language needed to understand the problem?   YES   NO
   If so, how?
   - ☐ by explaining vocabulary
   - ☐ by explaining sentence structure
   - ☐ other _____

6. Did the instructor check the level of student understanding before moving to the Practice Stage of the lesson?   YES   NO
   If so, how?
   - ☐ by asking questions that required nonverbal responses (hand signals, yes/no cards)
   - ☐ by eliciting answers from individual students
   - ☐ by moving around the room and checking
   - ☐ other _____

7. **Was the problem identified?**   YES   NO
   If so, how?
   - ☐ by the instructor telling the students
   - ☐ by students answering the instructor's questions
   - ☐ other _____

PRACTICE

8. **Were possible solutions to the problem identified?**   YES   NO
   If so, how?
   - ☐ individually
   - ☐ in pairs
   - ☐ in small groups
   - ☐ in the whole group

⑊⑊⑊⑊▶ FEEDBACK FORM (continued)

9. **Did the instructor provide opportunities for students to discuss the consequences of each solution?**   **YES   NO**

   If so, how?
   ☐ by providing materials to guide students (i.e., realia, visuals, worksheets)
   ☐ by using a variety of grouping strategies (i.e., whole group, small groups, pairs, individuals)
   ☐ by providing for more than one learning modality (i.e., kinesthetic, aural, oral, written)

10. Did the instructor monitor student practice?   YES   NO

    If so, how?
    ☐ by observing student participation in the practice
    ☐ by working with individuals/groups
    ☐ by moving around the room and observing
    ☐ other

11. **Was a solution to the problem selected?**   **YES   NO**

    If so, how?
    ☐ individually
    ☐ in pairs
    ☐ in small groups
    ☐ in the whole group

12. Did the instructor provide opportunities for the students to report back?   YES   NO

    If so, how?
    ☐ individually
    ☐ in pairs
    ☐ in small groups
    ☐ in the whole group

13. Did the instructor correct language errors only when there was a communication breakdown?   YES   NO

    If so, how?
    ☐ by providing correct responses
    ☐ by eliciting correct responses from individual students
    ☐ by eliciting the correct responses from all students
    ☐ by modeling the correct responses
    ☐ other

EVALUATION

14. Did the instructor assess individuals on the attainment of the objective?   YES   NO

    If so, how?
    ☐ by having students complete a written assignment
    ☐ by having students take a test
    ☐ by having students demonstrate the learning
    ☐ other

APPLICATION

15. Did the instructor provide an opportunity for the students to apply the material in a new situation relevant to their own life roles?   YES   NO

    If so, how?
    ☐ by having students provide responses based on their own experiences
    ☐ by having students interact with each other using their own words
    ☐ by having students complete an out-of-class assignment
    ☐ other

‣ FOLLOW-UP

Think about the video demonstration and review the Feedback Form. Then answer the questions and discuss your answers.

1. What did you find especially effective?

    _____

    _____

    _____

    _____

2. What did the students or teacher do that led you to this opinion?

    _____

    _____

    _____

    _____

Teacher Training Through Video
Copyright©1992 by Longman Publishing Group

Classroom Observation

Observing an actual class offers another model of the problem-solving technique. There are three parts to this Classroom Observation section. In the first part, *Lesson Focus*, you will identify basic information about the class observed. In the second part, *Feedback Form*, you will identify steps observed in the lesson. In the third part, *Follow-Up*, you will analyze and discuss the classroom observation.

▶ LESSON FOCUS

Observe a class in which the technique is used. Based on your observations, complete this form, describing the class and the lesson focus. Then complete the Feedback Form on pages 10 and 11. Pay special attention to the boldfaced key steps on the Feedback Form.

CLASS LEVEL: _____

LENGTH OF CLASS: _____ NUMBER OF STUDENTS: _____

LOCATION: _____ INSTRUCTOR: _____

TOPIC: _____

OBJECTIVE: The students will be able to _____

_____

_____

BASIC SKILLS (Language):

_____

_____

LIFE SKILLS (Content): _____

MAJOR SKILLS: Listening   Speaking   Reading   Writing

▶ FEEDBACK FORM ···▶ PROBLEM SOLVING

*Each question on the form refers to a step in the teaching process. For each question, decide whether you observed the behavior. If so, indicate what was observed by checking the appropriate box(es). Key steps in the technique are in **boldface.***

WARM-UP/REVIEW

1. Did the instructor relate the lesson objective to previous learning?   YES   NO
   If so, how?
   ☐ by having students practice previously studied material
   ☐ by providing a warm-up activity
   ☐ other _____

INTRODUCTION

2. Did the instructor focus student attention on the lesson?   YES   NO
   If so, how?
   ☐ by using visuals and/or realia
   ☐ by asking questions
   ☐ by describing a situation
   ☐ by telling a story
   ☐ other _____

3. Did the instructor establish the purpose of the lesson?   YES   NO
   If so, how?
   ☐ by stating the lesson objective
   ☐ by relating the lesson objective to the students' own lives
   ☐ other _____

PRESENTATION

4. **Was a problem situation provided?**   **YES   NO**
   If so, how?
   ☐ by using visuals and/or realia
   ☐ by explaining or describing
   ☐ by asking questions
   ☐ other _____

5. Did the instructor work with the language needed to understand the problem?   YES   NO
   If so, how?
   ☐ by explaining vocabulary
   ☐ by explaining sentence structure
   ☐ other _____

6. Did the instructor check the level of student understanding before moving to the Practice Stage of the lesson?   YES   NO
   If so, how?
   ☐ by asking questions that required nonverbal responses (hand signals, yes/no cards)
   ☐ by eliciting answers from individual students
   ☐ by moving around the room and checking
   ☐ other _____

7. **Was the problem identified?**   **YES   NO**
   If so, how?
   ☐ by the instructor telling the students
   ☐ by students answering the instructor's questions
   ☐ other _____

PRACTICE

8. **Were possible solutions to the problem identified?**   **YES   NO**
   If so, how?
   ☐ individually
   ☐ in pairs
   ☐ in small groups
   ☐ in the whole group

Teacher Training Through Video
Copyright©1992 by Longman Publishing Group

9. Did the instructor provide opportunities for students to discuss the consequences of each solution?   **YES NO**

If so, how?
- ☐ by providing materials to guide students (i.e., realia, visuals, worksheets)
- ☐ by using a variety of grouping strategies (i.e., whole group, small groups, pairs, individuals)
- ☐ by providing for more than one learning modality (i.e., kinesthetic, aural, oral, written)

10. Did the instructor monitor student practice?   YES NO

If so, how?
- ☐ by observing student participation in the practice
- ☐ by working with individuals/groups
- ☐ by moving around the room and observing
- ☐ other

11. Was a solution to the problem selected?   **YES NO**

If so, how?
- ☐ individually
- ☐ in pairs
- ☐ in small groups
- ☐ in the whole group

12. Did the instructor provide opportunities for the students to report back?   YES NO

If so, how?
- ☐ individually
- ☐ in pairs
- ☐ in small groups
- ☐ in the whole group

13. Did the instructor correct language errors only when there was a communication breakdown?   YES NO

If so, how?
- ☐ by providing correct responses
- ☐ by eliciting correct responses from individual students
- ☐ by eliciting the correct responses from all students
- ☐ by modeling the correct responses
- ☐ other

EVALUATION

14. Did the instructor assess individuals on the attainment of the objective?   YES NO

If so, how?
- ☐ by having students complete a written assignment
- ☐ by having students take a test
- ☐ by having students demonstrate the learning
- ☐ other

APPLICATION

15. Did the instructor provide an opportunity for the students to apply the material in a new situation relevant to their own life roles?   YES NO

If so, how?
- ☐ by having students provide responses based on their own experiences
- ☐ by having students interact with each other using their own words
- ☐ by having students complete an out-of-class assignment
- ☐ other

╫╫╫╫╫╫▸ FOLLOW-UP ▍▍▍▍▍▍▍▍▍▍▍▍▍▍▍▍▍▍▍▍▍▍▍▍▍▍▍▍▍▍▍▍▍

Think about your classroom observation and review the Feedback Form. Then answer the questions and discuss your answers.

1. What did you find especially effective?

   _____

   _____

   _____

   _____

2. What did the students or teacher do that led you to this opinion?

   _____

   _____

   _____

   _____

Guided Practice

The exercises that follow will give you practice in using the key steps in the problem-solving technique.

Think about the video demonstration and your classroom observation. Then use the information and Resource Materials that follow to complete the practice exercises.

TOPIC: *Male/Female roles*

OBJECTIVE: The students will be able to *identify the problems, possible solutions, and consequences of a husband and wife having conflicting views of the role of a wife and mother*

BASIC SKILLS (Language):

VOCABULARY: *Critical thinking skills*

Discussion skills

LIFE SKILLS (Content): *The role of a wife*

MAJOR SKILLS: (Listening) (Speaking) Reading Writing

RESOURCE MATERIALS

ANH AND TONG'S PROBLEM

Anh is a young housewife with two children. She and her husband Tong came to the United States four years ago. Tong is an assembler in a factory. He works hard and takes good care of his family. Sometimes he works seven days a week and he comes home very tired.

Anh has a lot of free time. The children go to school and they don't come home for lunch. Anh cooks breakfast and dinner. She cleans their small apartment, washes clothes, in a washing machine and she watches a lot of TV. Anh used to visit her friends and neighbors, but many are working now and some have moved away. She wants to go out on weekends, but Tong doesn't want to because he is working or he is too tired. Anh is lonely and bored.

Anh wants to learn to drive and wants to work. When she talks to Tong about this he gets angry. He doesn't have time to teach Anh to drive. He doesn't want to buy a second car. And he doesn't want Anh to work. He thinks a wife should stay at home and take care of the children while the husband goes to work.

┼┼┼┼┼┼┼► PRACTICE 1 ▌▌

···► KEY STEP: IDENTIFYING THE PROBLEM
FEEDBACK FORM, STEP 7

Read the questions asked on the video demonstration to lead students to identify the problem.

- ■ "So, the promotion, getting the higher job, is that the big problem? Or is the move the big problem?"
- ■ "He feels what?"
- ■ "She's thinking about the house? Maybe what else?"
- ■ "What's the problem with the move?"

Using the Resource Material on page 13, develop an activity or questions to lead your students to identify the problem. Write the problem you would like identified.

ACTIVITY OR QUESTIONS

_____

_____

_____

_____

_____

_____

PROBLEM TO IDENTIFY

_____

_____

_____

_____

_____

_____

PRACTICE 2

···▶ ## KEY STEP: IDENTIFYING POSSIBLE SOLUTIONS
FEEDBACK FORM, STEP 8

Read the question asked on the video demonstration to lead students to identify possible solutions. Then examine the solutions that were identified.

> "If the wife says I will not move, and the husband says okay, what do you think might happen?"

- ■ Solution 1: Decline job
- ■ Solution 2: Accept job and move with family
- ■ Solution 3: Accept job; husband moves; wife and family stay
- ■ Solution 4: Accept job; family moves halfway between job and school

Using the Resource Material on page 13, develop an activity or questions to lead students to identify possible solutions. List the solutions you would like identified.

ACTIVITY OR QUESTIONS

_____

_____

_____

_____

_____

_____

SOLUTIONS TO IDENTIFY

_____

_____

_____

_____

_____

_____

⊹⊹⊹⊹⊹⊹⊹▶ PRACTICE 3 ▐▐▐▐▐▐▐▐▐▐▐▐▐▐▐▐▐▐▐▐▐▐▐▐▐▐▐▐▐

⋯▶ KEY STEP: IDENTIFYING CONSEQUENCES TO SOLUTIONS
FEEDBACK FORM, STEP 9

Read the questions from the video demonstration designed to lead the students to identify the possible consequences of each solution identified. Then examine the consequences that were identified.

- ■ "So the move will make him, make the husband feel what?"
- ■ "Why does she feel happy about the promotion?"
- ■ "What does she have in San Diego?"

Solutions from page 15	Consequences
#1	No salary increase; no disruption
#2	More money; wife can't finish school
#3	More money; family split
#4	More money; family together; more commuting

Using the Resource Material on page 13, develop an activity or questions to lead students to identify possible consequences of the solutions you listed in Practice 2. List the consequences you would like identified.

ACTIVITY OR QUESTIONS

_____

_____

_____

_____

_____

CONSEQUENCES TO IDENTIFY

_____

_____

_____

_____

_____

 PRACTICE 4 |||||||||||||||||||||||||||||||||||||||||||||||||||||||||||||||||||||||||||

····▶ KEY STEP: SELECTING A SOLUTION
FEEDBACK FORM, STEP 11

Read the strategies from the video demonstration designed to lead the students (collectively or individually) to select the "best" solution.

- ■ Groups are formed, with five students in each group. Each person expresses his or her opinion as to the "best" solution, and the group reaches a consensus.

- ■ Students write letters to the woman with the problem suggesting their personal choice of the "best" solution.

Using the Resource Material on page 13, develop an activity to lead students to select the "best" solution.

ACTIVITY FOR GROUPS

_____

_____

_____

_____

_____

_____

ACTIVITY FOR INDIVIDUALS

_____

_____

_____

_____

_____

_____

Teacher Training Through Video
Copyright©1992 by Longman Publishing Group

PROBLEM SOLVING   17

 PRACTICE 5

···▶ KEY STEP: PROVIDING A PROBLEM SITUATION
FEEDBACK FORM, STEP 4

The problem-solving technique uses students' concerns and problems as subjects for discussion. Published materials with problem-solving activities may not include ones relevant to your students. Moreover, the most effective problem-solving lessons are ones in which the problems and concerns discussed are based on those of students in the class. To write a problem-solving story for your students, follow these guidelines.

- Identify a problem that one of your students has had.
- Use fictitious names to avoid embarrassment.
- Use clear, simple language that is appropriate to students' level of English.
- Select a problem that is not impossible. If it cannot be solved, there should be some possibility for improvement of the situation.
- Do not provide a solution.

Using a problem or concern of a student, write a story.

_____

_____

_____

_____

_____

_____

_____

_____

_____

_____

_____

_____

_____

Application

The exercises that follow will give you an opportunity to transfer the skills you have acquired to your own classroom. They will guide you in focusing the lesson, planning the lesson, and evaluating the lesson.

▶ LESSON FOCUS

Plan a lesson that uses the problem-solving technique. Use this form to focus the lesson.

CLASS LEVEL: _____

LENGTH OF CLASS: _____ NUMBER OF STUDENTS: _____

LOCATION: _____ INSTRUCTOR: _____

TOPIC: _____

OBJECTIVE: The students will be able to _____

_____

_____

BASIC SKILLS (Language):

_____

_____

LIFE SKILLS (Content): _____

MAJOR SKILLS: Listening   Speaking   Reading   Writing

RESOURCE MATERIALS

▌▌▌▌▌▌▌▌▶ LESSON PLAN ▌▌▌▌▌▌▌▌▌▌▌▌▌▌▌▌▌▌▌▌▌▌▌▌▌▌▌▌▌▌▌▌▌

The following steps are on the Feedback Form. Describe how you will include them in your lesson. Plan at least one activity for each step.

Step 1:	Relate the lesson objective to previous learning.
Step 2:	Focus student attention on the lesson.
Step 3:	Establish the purpose of the lesson.
Step 4:	Provide a problem situation.
Step 5:	Work with the language needed to understand the problem.
Step 6:	Check the level of student understanding.
Step 7:	Have students identify the problem.
Step 8:	Have students identify possible solutions.
Step 9:	Allow opportunities for students to discuss the consequences of each proposed solution.
Step 10:	Identify how you will monitor the practice.
Step 11:	Have students select a solution.
Step 12:	Allow students to "report back" if small group, pair, or individual work was included.
Step 13:	Identify how you will provide feedback when there is a communication breakdown.
Step 14:	Identify how you will assess individual students on the attainment of the objective.
Step 15:	Provide an opportunity for students to apply the material to a new situation.

▶ LESSON EVALUATION ... PROBLEM SOLVING

Teach your lesson. Then use the Feedback Form to evaluate your lesson.

WARM-UP/REVIEW

1. Did the instructor relate the lesson objective to previous learning?   YES   NO

   If so, how?
   - ☐ by having students practice previously studied material
   - ☐ by providing a warm-up activity
   - ☐ other

INTRODUCTION

2. Did the instructor focus student attention on the lesson?   YES   NO

   If so, how?
   - ☐ by using visuals and/or realia
   - ☐ by asking questions
   - ☐ by describing a situation
   - ☐ by telling a story
   - ☐ other

3. Did the instructor establish the purpose of the lesson?   YES   NO

   If so, how?
   - ☐ by stating the lesson objective
   - ☐ by relating the lesson objective to the students' own lives
   - ☐ other

PRESENTATION

4. **Was a problem situation provided?**   YES   NO

   If so, how?
   - ☐ by using visuals and/or realia
   - ☐ by explaining or describing
   - ☐ by asking questions
   - ☐ other

5. Did the instructor work with the language needed to understand the problem?   YES   NO

   If so, how?
   - ☐ by explaining vocabulary
   - ☐ by explaining sentence structure
   - ☐ other

6. Did the instructor check the level of student understanding before moving to the Practice Stage of the lesson?   YES   NO

   If so, how?
   - ☐ by asking questions that required nonverbal responses (hand signals, yes/no cards)
   - ☐ by eliciting answers from individual students
   - ☐ by moving around the room and checking
   - ☐ other

7. **Was the problem identified?**   **YES**   **NO**

   If so, how?
   - ☐ by the instructor telling the students
   - ☐ by students answering the instructor's questions
   - ☐ other

PRACTICE

8. **Were possible solutions to the problem identified?**   **YES**   **NO**

   If so, how?
   - ☐ individually
   - ☐ in pairs
   - ☐ in small groups
   - ☐ in the whole group

9. Did the instructor provide opportunities for the students to discuss the consequences of each solution?   **YES**   **NO**

If so, how?
- ☐ by providing materials to guide students (i.e., realia, visuals, worksheets)
- ☐ by using a variety of grouping strategies (i.e., whole group, small groups, pairs, individuals)
- ☐ by providing for more than one learning modality (i.e., kinesthetic, aural, oral, written)

10. Did the instructor monitor student practice?   YES   NO

If so, how?
- ☐ by observing student participation in the practice
- ☐ by working with individuals/groups
- ☐ by moving around the room and observing
- ☐ other _____

11. Was a solution to the problem selected?   **YES**   **NO**

If so, how?
- ☐ individually
- ☐ in pairs
- ☐ in small groups
- ☐ in the whole group

12. Did the instructor provide opportunities for the students to report back?   YES   NO

If so, how?
- ☐ individually
- ☐ in pairs
- ☐ in small groups
- ☐ in the whole group

13. Did the instructor correct language errors only when there was a communication breakdown?   YES   NO

If so, how?
- ☐ by providing the correct responses
- ☐ by eliciting the correct responses from individual students
- ☐ by eliciting the correct responses from all students
- ☐ by modeling the correct responses
- ☐ other _____

EVALUATION

14. Did the instructor assess individuals on the attainment of the objective?   YES   NO

If so, how?
- ☐ by having students complete a written assignment
- ☐ by having students take a test
- ☐ by having students demonstrate the learning
- ☐ other _____

APPLICATION

15. Did the instructor provide an opportunity for the students to apply the material in a new situation relevant to their own life roles?   YES   NO

If so, how?
- ☐ by having students provide responses based on their own experiences
- ☐ by having students interact with each other using their own words
- ☐ by having students complete an out-of-class assignment
- ☐ other _____

⊩⊩⊩⊩⊩▶ FOLLOW-UP ▮▮▮▮▮▮▮▮▮▮▮▮▮▮▮▮▮▮▮▮▮▮▮▮▮

Think about your lesson and review the Feedback Form. Then answer the questions and discuss your answers.

1. What did you find especially effective?

    _____

    _____

    _____

    _____

2. What did the students do that led you to this opinion?

    _____

    _____

    _____

    _____

3. If you taught the lesson again, would you do anything differently? If so, what? Why?

    _____

    _____

    _____

    _____

Appendix

⊪⊪⊪⊪⊪▶ VIDEO INSTRUCTIONAL MATERIALS ▮▮▮▮▮▮▮▮▮▮▮▮

⋯▶ LEE AND MAY'S PROBLEM

Lee and his family came to the United States about seven years ago. Lee was a mechanic in his country and is now working in the tire department of a large store. His wife, May, is an assistant in a beauty shop and is going to cosmetology school. She will get her license next August. May's sister, who lives next door to them, takes care of Lee and May's children while they are at work. Lee and May are very happy in San Diego, because they have many relatives and friends who live here.

Last week, Lee's boss told him that he will open a store near Oceanside (about 60 miles from San Diego). He wants Lee to be the manager of the new tire department. Lee was so happy. He went home and told his wife and children about the promotion and that they will move to Oceanside next month. He thought that they would be proud and happy, but they were upset.

What's wrong? What's the problem? What should Lee and May do? Please give them some good advice. Tell them what to do.

_____

_____

_____

_____

_____

_____

_____

_____

_____

_____

Developed by Linda Little, San Diego Community College District

◀▮▮▮▮▮▮▮▶ VIDEO LESSON PLAN ▮▮▮▮▮▮▮▮▮▮▮▮▮▮▮▮▮▮▮▮▮▮▮▮▮▮▮▮▮▮▮▮▮▮

Objective	To decide whether or not to accept a promotion that requires a move to another area.
Materials Needed:	Handout (reading)
Length of Lesson:	Approximately 1 hour and 25 minutes

TIME FRAME	STEPS ON THE FEEDBACK FORM
2 to 3 minutes	**Steps 1 to 4:** Explain where the problem came from and give students a copy of the story.
15 minutes	**Step 5:** Tell students to read the problem silently and ask them to identify vocabulary they do not understand.
3 to 5 minutes	**Step 6:** Ask some questions to see if students understand the story. Relate the story to the students' own lives by asking questions about similar situations in their native countries.
10 minutes	**Step 7:** Ask students to identify the problem(s) and list them on the chalkboard (the promotion and the move).
25 minutes	**Step 8:** Have students identify and discuss possible solutions (move now, move later, move half way between two towns) either as a whole group or in small groups, depending on the level of the class and their experience with problem solving.
15 minutes	**Steps 9 to 11:** Divide students into small groups of four to six students. Ask them to share their solutions, identify consequences of each, and reach a consensus if possible. Move among groups and assist as needed.
5 minutes	**Step 12:** Have one person from each group report back to the whole class the decision(s) of the group.
	Step 13: Throughout the Practice Stage (Steps 8 to 12), correct errors only when there is a communication breakdown. For other errors (e.g., pronunciation, structure), repeat the students' responses using correct English without pointing out error.
10 minutes	**Step 14:** Have individuals write a letter to the student who has a problem and offer their own solutions. Collect the papers to obtain input on the effectiveness of the problem-solving process and the language difficulties encountered.

Developed by Linda Little, San Diego Community College District

⋯▶ ACKNOWLEDGMENTS

This series was originally developed by the ESL Teacher Institute through a contract with the Association of California School Administrators, Foundation for Educational Administration. Major funding for the project was received from the Adult Education Unit of the Youth, Adult, and Alternative Education Division of the California Department of Education.

Special thanks to the following groups of people:

> To the more than sixty trainers in California since the inception of the project for their input toward refinement of the materials

> To the adult school administrators in California for their support of faculty who served as regional trainers and as demonstration teachers

> To the consultants in the Adult Education Unit of the California Department of Education for their enthusiasm in promoting the training

> To the ACSA staff for cheerfully accepting the additional work that resulted

Special thanks to the following individuals:

> To Judy Alamprese for her design of an evaluation study that collected data on the teaching behaviors of fifty instructors pre- and post-training and for her interpretation of the data from the study, which contributed to extensive revisions of the training materials

> To Cindy Ranii for her work in adapting the materials for independent study, which contributed to further refinement

> To Autumn Keltner for her belief in and support of the project during its initial stages and for her innumerable classroom observations during the evaluation study

> To John Opalka, Cathleen Calice, and Julie Raquel for their dedication to the project and the quality of their work as project assistants

> To Jane Zinner for her guidance as project administrator

> To Edda Caraballo-Browne, Ray Eberhard, Bob Ehlers, Carlos Gonzalez, and Dick Stiles for their assistance in the development and dissemination of the project's materials

> To Penny Laporte for the insights she brings through the editing process

> To Joanne Dresner for her professional commitment to this project

···▸ TITLES IN THE TEACHER TRAINING THROUGH VIDEO SERIES

- ## *THE COMPLETE SET:*   78771

    The set includes the ten videos and corresponding reproducible masters; a loose-leaf binder for the reproducible masters; a User's Guide; and a carrying case.

- ## *PROGRAM COMPONENTS:*

ORDER CODE

- Lesson Planning
    Video and reproducible masters   78741
    Workbook   78761
- Focused Listening
    Video and reproducible masters   78742
    Workbook   78762
- Early Production
    Video and reproducible masters   78743
    Workbook   78763
- Dialogue/Drill
    Video and reproducible masters   78744
    Workbook   78764
- Information Gap
    Video and reproducible masters   78745
    Workbook   78765
- Role Play
    Video and reproducible masters   78746
    Workbook   78766
- Problem Solving
    Video and reproducible masters   78747
    Workbook   78767
- Language Experience
    Video and reproducible masters   78748
    Workbook   78768
- Life Skills Reading
    Video and reproducible masters   78749
    Workbook   78769
- Narrative Reading
    Video and reproducible masters   78750
    Workbook   78770
- Also Available
    User's Guide   78947